Highlights

Easter Puzzles
Puzzle Mania

HIGHLIGHTS PRESS
Honesdale, Pennsylvania

Contents

When you finish a puzzle, check it off √.
Good luck, and happy puzzling!

A-Mazing!

Word Play

Hidden Pictures

Look Twice

Do the Math

Easter Egg-stras

Candy Counter

No need to sugarcoat it, this is a sweet puzzle! Each of these candy names will fit into the grid in just one way. Use a word's length as a clue for where to put it. When you've filled them all in, write the letters in the shaded boxes in order in the spaces below to see the answer to the riddle.

What crop does a farmer with a sweet tooth grow?

Word list

GUM	LICORICE
~~MINT~~	LOLLIPOP
FUDGE	CANDY CANE
TAFFY	JELLY BEAN
CARAMEL	CHOCOLATE BAR
TRUFFLE	PEANUT BRITTLE

Hidden Pictures
Hopping Egg Hunt

sock

bowl

paintbrush

spoon

banana

toothbrush

frog

glove

Meet the Beetles

Mingo is meeting up with his friends. They've all made it to the middle of the maze. Can you help Mingo find his way there?

Start

Finish

Illustrated by Mattia Cerato

Easter Basket Hunt

Illustrated by Amanda Enright

Check...and Double Check

How many differences do you see between these pictures?

11

WHAT'S THE BUZZ?

We don't mean to bug you. But we do want you to search for the **35** insects hiding in this grid. Look for them up, down, across, backwards, and diagonally. How many can you spot?

Word list

~~APHID~~	KATYDID
BEDBUG	LADYBUG
BEETLE	LEAFHOPPER
BLOWFLY	LOCUST
BUTTERFLY	LOUSE
CICADA	MANTIS
COCKROACH	MAYFLY
CRICKET	MEALYBUG
DRAGONFLY	MIDGE
EARWIG	MOSQUITO
FIRE ANT	MOTH
FIREFLY	SILVERFISH
FLEA	STINKBUG
FRUIT FLY	TERMITE
GNAT	WALKING STICK
GRASSHOPPER	WEEVIL
HONEYBEE	
HORNET	
HOUSEFLY	

```
T E F R U I T F L Y Y L F E R I F
E E B U Z Z T S I L V E R F I S H H
R B M N E T M E A L Y B U G O X K
M Y N Y S A L J N C R I C K E T L
I E U U C O C K R O A C H F G E A
T N U L O D D R A G O N F L Y U B F
E O F Y F W O L B R H K P G B H
L H B G U B K N I T S V A H K Y H
E B E D B U G X A W Y U T O W D A
K L Y M B U T T E R F L Y U H A P
M A Y F L Y A V L S R X D S I L P
P D R O N E N V F M X V I E R E E
W A L K I N G S T I C K D F R O R S
E W E E V I L E A N V I J L U T S
C A P H E E L G H C M S C Y G P I
H P R C V T D T O F I R E A N T T
I H X W E V O E G D I M D U D V N
R I T E I M O S Q U I T O H N A A
P D B Y P G R A S S H O P P E R M
```

Spring Cleaning

Squirrels love a clean park. Can you clean up this puzzle?
Find the hidden objects.

magnet

fish

cane

14

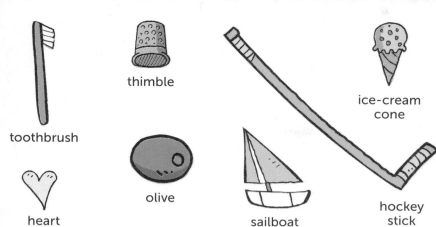

toothbrush

thimble

ice-cream cone

bat

comb

heart

olive

sailboat

hockey stick

spoon

cat

A Real Nut

Each of the pairs below has the name of a real nut and a fake one. Which is which? Go nuts and circle the real nuts. We did one to get you started.

~~Mustachios~~
(Pistachios)

Peanuts
Beenuts

Walnuts
Floornuts

Toucans
Pecans

Brazil Nuts
Baltimore Nuts

Legnuts
Chestnuts

Cashews
Achoos

Macadamia Nuts
Academic Nuts

Illustrated by Neil Numberman

Hidden * * Pieces

Can you find the seven jigsaw pieces in this photo of Easter eggs?

What's Wrong?

How many silly things can you find in this picture?

Illustrated by Julissa Mora

19

Illustrated by Jackie Stafford

crescent moon

bowl

cupcake

envelope

button

adhesive bandage

toucan

candle

toothbrush

bell

kite

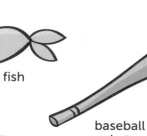
fish

baseball bat

banana

teacup

20

Splish Splash

Find the hidden objects in the rainy scene on the left. Then fill in the umbrella puzzle with words from the WORD LIST on this page.

Use the number of letters in each word as a clue to where it might fit. We filled in one word to get you started.

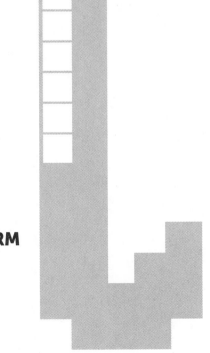

WORD LIST

5 LETTERS
BOOTS
CLOUD

6 LETTERS
PUDDLE
SHOWER
SPLASH

7 LETTERS
DRIZZLE
RAINBOW

8 LETTERS
DOWNPOUR
RAINCOAT
RAINDROP
~~UMBRELLA~~

12 LETTERS
THUNDERSTORM

Flower Q's

Jumbled Flowers

Unscramble each set of letters to get the name of a flower.

YILL __ __ __ __

LITUP __ __ __ __ __ __

ICALL __ __ __ __ __

LOVEIT __ __ __ __ __ __

FADIFOLD __ __ __ __ __ __ __ __

Guess What?

What two flowers are mixed in the picture below?

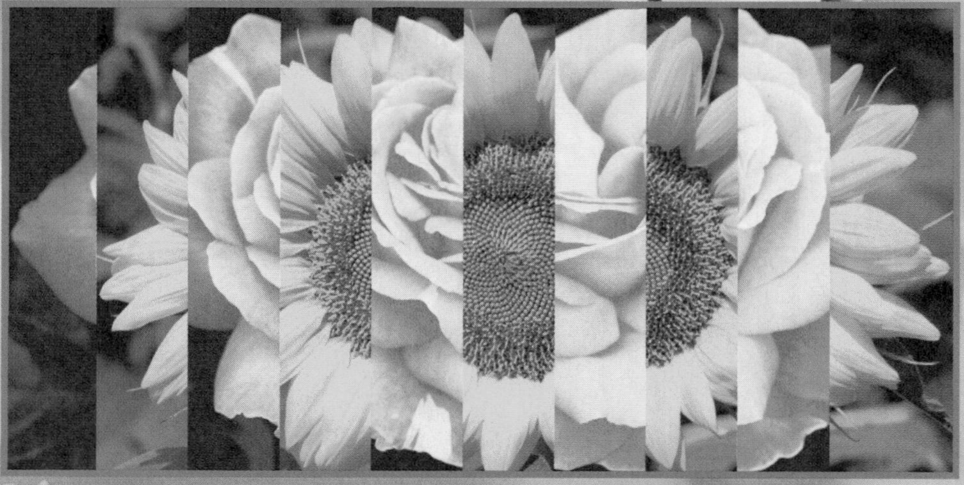

Flower Girl Power

Flora is the flower girl in her aunt Lily's wedding. Can you help Flora lead the way down the aisle?

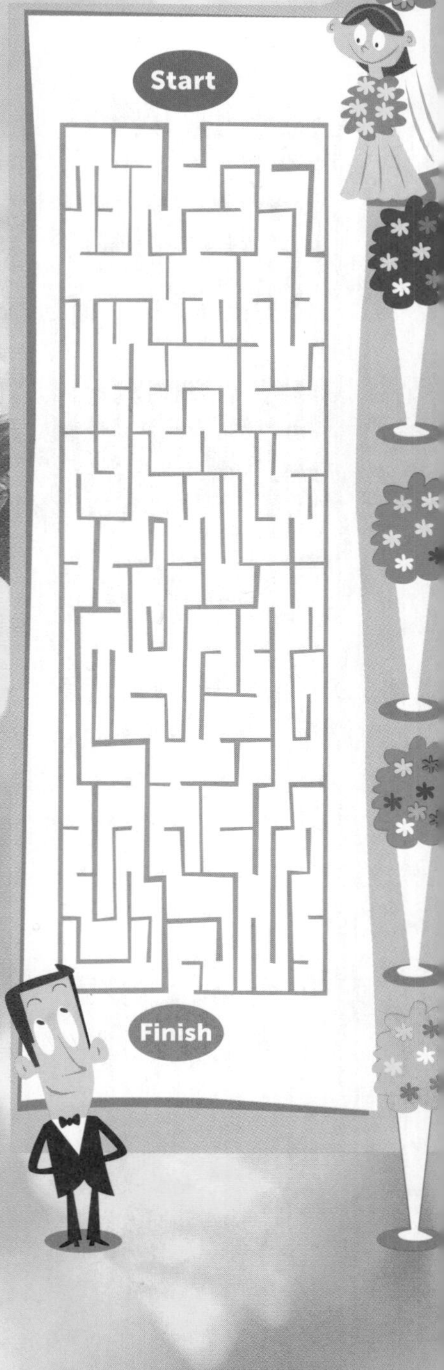

Start

Finish

Hidden Flowers

A flower is hidden in the letters of each sentence. Find **ASTER** in the first one. Then find a different flower in each of the others.

As Terry says, vanilla is better than chocolate.

A superhero seldom fails.

Ms. Gorda is your new teacher.

This fir is taller than it was last year.

On the porch, I don't get sunburned.

Flower or Not?

Each pair of words has one flower and one faker. Circle the flowers.

Bluebell or Barbell?

Snapdragon or Snickerdoodle?

Chrysalis or Chrysanthemum?

Rhododendron or Rapscallion?

Gladiolus or Gondola?

Clementine or Clematis?

Hydra or Hydrangea?

Foxglove or Bearclaw?

Flower Discovery

More than 100,000 flower species have been discovered on Earth, and many more are yet to be found. If you discovered a new kind of flower, what would it look like? Draw it here.

Crafts

Eggs-traordinary Art

By Julie Crabtree

1. Cover your work area with **newspaper**.

2. Lay sheets of **wax paper** on top. Pour small pools of non-toxic **paint** onto the paper.

3. Roll **hard-boiled eggs** through the paint. Let them dry. Keep the eggs refrigerated.

Easter Mosaics

By Jean Kuhn

1. Cover **corrugated cardboard** with **colored paper**. Tape a **yarn** hanger to the back.

2. With a **pencil**, lightly draw a simple shape on the paper, such as an egg or a cross.

3. Fill the shape by gluing pieces of clean, **dyed eggshells**.

4. Add a paper border as a decoration.

Easter Wreath By Clare Mishica

1. Cut out a large circle from **thin cardboard**. Draw a smaller circle about 1 inch inside the edge of the first circle. Cut out the center circle and discard it.

2. Cut scrap **fabric** into 2-inch-by-7-inch strips.

3. Tie the fabric strips around the circle until it is covered. Trim the ends of the strips.

4. Cut a cross from **cardstock**. Punch a hole in the top. Tie it to the wreath with **yarn**. Tie a **ribbon** hanger on the wreath.

Craft samples by Buff McAllister. Photos by Hank Schneider.

Bunny Basket

By Ellen Javernick

1. Draw the pattern (below) twice onto **cardstock**. Cut them out. Use **markers** to draw faces.

2. Overlap the two patterns facedown to make an X. Glue the center squares together.

3. Fold the rabbit heads upward. Glue the edges together to form a basket. Let it dry.

4. Fill the basket with **Easter grass** and treats.

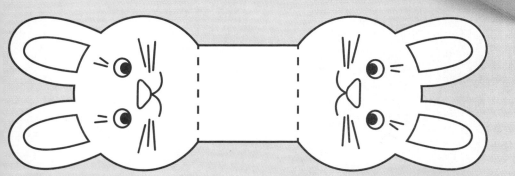

Grow Your Own Easter Grass!

By Jean Kuhn

1. Ten or more days before Easter, line the bottom and sides of an **Easter basket** with **plastic wrap**. Add a layer of **small stones** for drainage.

2. On top of the stones, add a layer of **potting soil** two inches deep. Moisten the soil so that it's damp but not soggy. Use about ¼ cup of **water** for every two cups of potting soil you've used.

3. Sprinkle a layer of fast-growing **grass seed** on the soil; the seeds should be close together. Cover them with a thin layer of potting soil.

4. Lay a sheet of plastic wrap over the soil to keep it moist. Set the basket near a sunny window.

5. In two to three days, when the seeds sprout, remove the plastic covering. Water the grass lightly as needed. Trim it with scissors, if you'd like. Trim away any plastic that extends above the edge of the basket.

Sock Bunny

By Robin M. Adams

1. Stuff the foot part of **two socks** with **fiberfill** or **cotton balls**.

2. With **string**, tie the socks together in three places to create feet, a body, a head, and ears.

3. Glue on **wiggle eyes**, a **pompom** nose, **chenille-stick** whiskers, and a cotton-ball tail. Tie a **ribbon** around the neck.

25

Hidden Pictures
Eggs for Breakfast

Can you find these 12 hidden objects in this henhouse?

teacup

lion's head

canoe

balloon

rolling pin

flag

ice-cream cone

light bulb

broccoli

zipper

umbrella

basketball

Dot to Dot

Connect the dots from 1 to 24 to find another animal that lives on a farm.

Illustrated by Ron Lieser

WIGGLE PICTURES

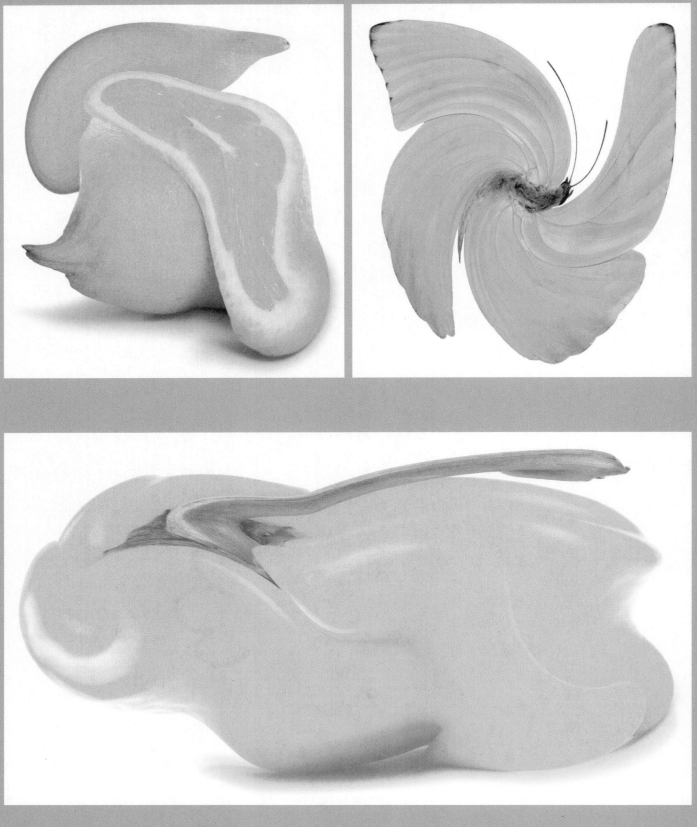

These yellow things have been twisted and turned.
Can you figure out what each one is?

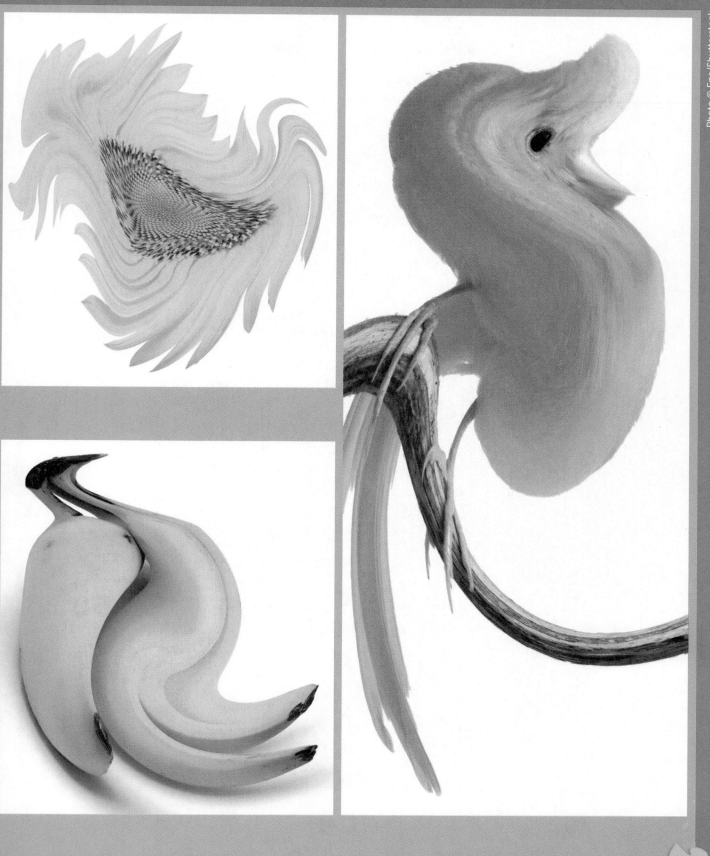

Hundred Hop

Help Hilda hop across to any exit. Hilda can count only by 10s. She must hop across each number from 10 to 100 in order only once, and she can't cross back over her trail.

10   10

30   20   20   20

30

50   40   50

40

60   50   50   100

70

80   50   70

80   60   90

90

60   90   90   80

100

Illustrated by David Helton

Use your crayons, pencils, or markers to draw this rabbit.

1.

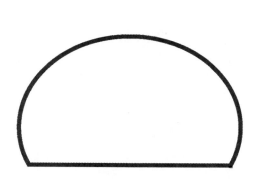

2.

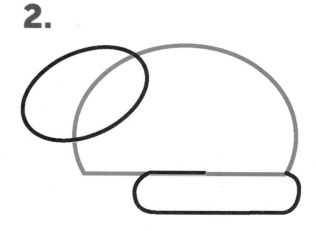

3.

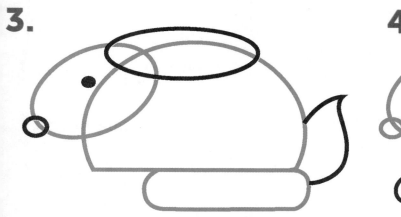

4.

5.

Illustrated by Ron Zalme

Shelled Out

These six eggs have just hatched. Follow the path from each shell to find out who—or what—hatched from each.

33

Hippity-Zippity

M

Look for each object below in the picture. Write the letters you find near each object in the spaces in order to answer the joke. Hop to it!

I

S

O

T

H

P

A

What do you call a happy bunny?

☐ ☐ ☐ ☐ ☐ ☐ ☐ ☐ ☐ ☐

Hidden Pictures
Bunny Delivery

drum

peanut

mushroom

thimble

crayon

domino

sailboat

fish

flashlight

mallet

slice of pie

acorn

teacup

open book

35

Matching Eggs

**Each Easter egg in this picture has one that looks exactly like it.
Can you find all 16 matching pairs?**

Win by a Hare

Has the judge found the winner?
Can you find the hidden objects?

football

fish

turtle

yo-yo

pail

plunger

STATE FAIR
CARROT-GROWING CONTEST

JUDGE
1

bat

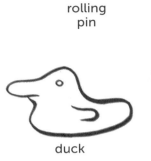
rolling pin

drumstick

pair of pants

cherries

duck

ladle

bowling pin

baseball cap

Healthy or Not?

There's one real vegetable in each pair of words below. Circle the real veggie. We did the first one for you.

Beeps
(Beets)

Celery
Salary

Cauliflower
Collie flower

Turndown
Turnip

Bunion
Onion

Asparagus
Asparaguts

Bok choy
Choc boy

Mini bagel
Rutabaga

Illustrated by Jef Czekaj

Bloomin' Eggs

These 20 spring surprises are hiding in this grid. Look for them up, down, across, backwards, and diagonally.

Word List

BONNET

BUNNY

CANDY

CHICKS

CHOCOLATE

DAFFODIL

DECORATE

DUCKLING

EGG HUNT

EGGS

FAMILY

HOP

JELLY BEANS

LAMB

LILY

MARSHMALLOW

NEST

ROBIN'S EGG

SPRING

TULIP

```
A S M Z F N Y W B B U N N Y N M P
G H R F R L R O G D D B O N N E T
O F B P I U Y G R W A S G Z R K D
W A C L O Q E O T P F N E P O Q C
T M E C N S F U P F F P W P W H S
E I C H N B F H J I O U R M T O P
Z L E I U S C C A N D Y H E N P R
D Y B C I B H Y B I I N E U C T I
G O E K M C O U H L J V T U D N
R C U S D E C O R A T E D E J U G
H I R D C U O L G M E F S G S C R
H H S S M Q L I M B F W R G V K I
T C N M S V A I O F I D G H M L T
U D D J V Z T P C F L E K U L I Z
L G P K V R E Y N E S T R N K N B
I J E L L Y B E A N S U K T B G O
P M A R S H M A L L O W J S V K S
```

Eggscruciating

Don't be chicken. Gather up all the clues you need to decode these riddles. Each colored egg stands for the capital letter on the egg box. Match the eggs with the letters to solve the code.

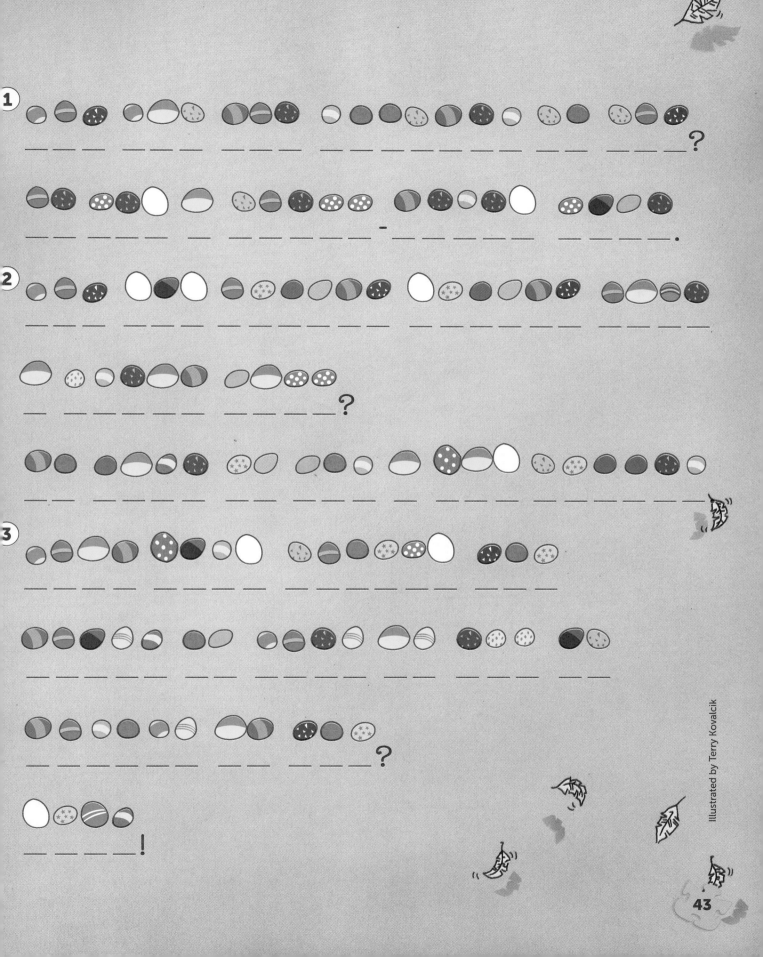

Hidden Pictures
Get on Board

heart

carrot

bowling ball

golf club

broccoli

envelope

wishbone

colander

slice of watermelon

lollipop

magnet

glove

spool of thread

crown

football

belt

doughnut

domino

button

cookie

What's Wrong?

How many silly things can you find in this picture?

MAKE A RAIN STICK

With Crafts Expert Jessie Messi!

You need:

- paper
- scissors
- a paper towel tube
- tape
- two handfuls of uncooked rice
- two chenille sticks
- markers or decorations (stickers, glitter, etc.)

1 Cut two squares of paper large enough to cover the ends of the paper towel tube. Tape one square over one end of the tube.

2 Pour two handfuls of uncooked rice into the tube.

3 Fold two chenille sticks accordion-style. Slide them into the paper towel tube.

4 Tape the second square of paper over the other end of the tube.

5 Decorate the tube.

6 Slowly tilt the rain stick back and forth to create the sound of rain.

coffeepot

hot dog

flashlight

trowel

pencil

umbrella

glove

tack

strawberry

paper airplane

jar

fork

ring

dog bone

cheese

candle

mug

Illustrated by Kelly Kennedy

47

Check...and Double Check

How many differences do you see between these pictures?

Double Cross

Try to keep your cool while solving this puzzle. To find the answer to the riddle below, first cross out all the pairs of matching letters. Then write the remaining letters in order in the spaces at the bottom of the page.

TT	BB	CC	AA	TH	PP	QQ
SS	EY	LL	XX	HA	KK	VV
VE	YY	DD	OO	BB	HA	GG
MM	RE	FF	EE	LL	II	CO
BB	QQ	AA	SS	ND	RR	ZZ
IT	CC	HH	PP	UU	IO	JJ
II	NI	XX	LL	RR	NG	WW

Illustrated by Dave Clegg

Why don't rabbits get hot in the summertime?

_ _ _ _   _ _ _ _

_ _ _ _-_ _ _ _ _ _ _ _ _ _ _ _ .

50

Tic Tac Row

Each of these umbrellas has something in common with the other two umbrellas in the same row. For example, in the top row across each umbrella is blue. Look at the other rows across, down, and diagonally. Can you tell what's alike in each row?

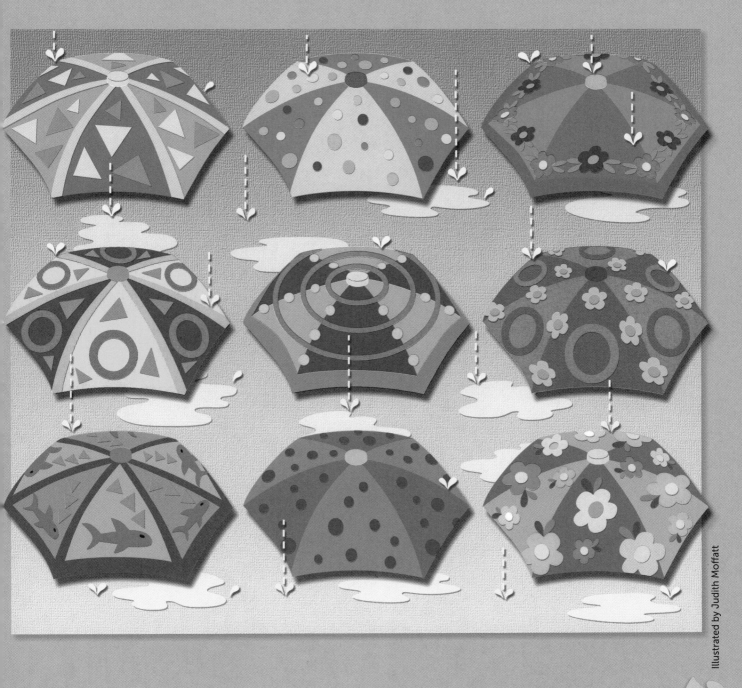

Illustrated by Judith Moffatt

Rabbit Search

Can you find 10 rabbits in this scene?

Illustrated by Alessandra Psacharopulo

53

Kite Plight

Hang on tight! These kite flyers have gotten their strings tangled. Follow each person's string to find out which kite he or she is flying.

Illustrated by Brian White

Puddle Play

Use the clues to figure out each duck's name. Good luck!

1. Dexter is wearing glasses.
2. Daphne likes wearing her hood up.
3. Duncan and Dylan are wearing rain boots.
4. Delilah's umbrella is the same color as her raincoat.
5. Dylan likes polka dots.

Hidden Pictures
Egg Factory

drinking straw

lollipop

ruler

wedge of orange

button

hockey stick

paper clip

horseshoe

harmonica

UFO

book

dustpan

ladle

waffle

mushroom

Crafts

Easter Garlands

By Edna Harrington

1. Cut shapes from **colored paper**. Decorate both sides of each shape with **stickers**, **markers**, and paper details. Punch a hole in each shape.

2. Knot three 6-foot-long pieces of **yarn** together at one end. Tape the knot to a worktable. Braid the yarn, then knot the other end.

3. Use yarn to tie the shapes onto the braided yarn.

Lovely Lilies

By Lauren Michaels

1. Trace the outlines of one adult's hand and one child's hand onto **colored paper**. Use a **marker** to outline each shape. Cut them out.

2. Glue the base of the small shape to the base of the large shape.

3. Roll the shapes together to form a flower, and tape the bottom, leaving a small hole.

4. Color a **wooden skewer** for a flower stem, and slide it into the hole. Tape it in place.

5. Cut two leaves from paper, outline them with a marker, and tape them to the stem.

Photos by Hank Schneider, Katharine Brown, Dave Justice, Guy Cali Associates, Inc., and Ken Karp. Craft samples by Buff McAllister.

Bunny-Cup Races

By JoAnn Markway

1. For each bunny cup, make ears from **chenille sticks** and **colored paper**. Glue or tape the ears to a **plastic cup**. Add **wiggle eyes**, a paper bow tie, and a **pompom** nose and tail. Draw a face with **markers**.

2. Make a bunny cup for each player.

To Play: Divide players into two teams. Form two lines. Choose a tree or other marker about 20 feet away as a turnaround spot. Put a **plastic Easter egg** in the cup of the first player on each team. At the start of the race, the first player on each team hops to the tree, touches it, then hops back. He or she then dumps the egg into the next player's cup without touching the egg. The first team to finish wins!

Easter-Egg Animals

By Marie E. Cecchini

1. From **craft foam**, cut out an animal's head, feet, and wings, if necessary.

2. Glue on **wiggle eyes** and decorate the face.

3. For legs, cut strips of **paper** and fold them accordion-style.

4. Glue a foot to each leg. Glue the legs to a **plastic egg**. Glue on the head (and wings).

Colorful Easter Cards

Cross with Lilies

By Anna Safsten

1. Cut out two rectangles from **cardstock**. Round the top edges. **Tape** the rectangles together at the top.

2. Cut out flowers and a cross from **craft foam**. Glue them to the front of the card. Decorate the card with **markers**.

Easter Basket

By April Theis

1. Fold a piece of **cardstock** in half. Cut out a half circle from the middle of the folded edge. Decorate the card with **glitter glue**.

2. Cut out eggs from **craft foam**. Glue them to the inside edge of the half circle. Glue **Easter grass** around the eggs.

3. Tape a **chenille-stick** handle to the back of the card. Cut out a tag from cardstock. Use a **marker** to write "Happy Easter" on it. Punch a hole in one end and tie it to the handle with **yarn**.

Bountiful Bouquets

A sweet-smelling shipment has arrived at Blossom's Flower Shop. Two bouquets have already been put in vases. It is up to you to help Blossom arrange the rest.

Here is the trick. The total number of flowers across, down, and diagonally must add up to 21. Keep the bunches together. Write the number of flowers that must go into each of the vases on Blossom's shelves.

What's Wrong?

How many silly things can you find in this picture?

Illustrated by Richard Torrey

Hidden Pictures
Hop to the Finish Line

teacup

tomato

sweet potato

whale

bell

musical note

envelope

crescent moon

snake

pencil

acorn

cookie

feather

seashell

nail

banana

heart

vase

Bird Words

Write the name of each bird on the blanks next to it. Then write the letters on the blanks with the matching numbers to find the answer to the riddle below.

$\overline{}_1 \ \overline{}_2 \ \overline{}_3 \ \overline{}_4 \ \overline{}_5$

$\overline{}_3 \ \overline{}_6 \ \overline{}_7 \ \overline{}_8 \ \overline{}_9 \ \overline{}_{10} \ \overline{}_{11}$

$\overline{}_{12} \ \overline{}_{10} \ \overline{}_1 \ \overline{}_1 \ \overline{}_2 \ \overline{}_{13}$

$\overline{}_{14} \ \overline{}_{12} \ \overline{}_{10} \ \overline{}_1 \ \overline{}_1 \ \overline{}_2 \ \overline{}_{15}$

$\overline{}_{16} \ \overline{}_7 \ \overline{}_{17} \ \overline{}_{17} \ \overline{}_4 \ \overline{}_5 \ \overline{}_{18} \ \overline{}_3 \ \overline{}_4 \ \overline{}_1 \ \overline{}_{19}$

Why is the sky so high?

$\overline{}_{14} \ \overline{}_2 \quad \overline{}_3 \ \overline{}_4 \ \overline{}_1 \ \overline{}_{19} \ \overline{}_{14} \quad \overline{}_{15} \ \overline{}_2 \ \overline{}_5 \ \overline{}_{13}$

$\overline{}_3 \ \overline{}_7 \ \overline{}_{17} \ \overline{}_{12} \quad \overline{}_{13} \ \overline{}_{16} \ \overline{}_8 \ \overline{}_4 \ \overline{}_1 \quad \overline{}_{16} \ \overline{}_8 \ \overline{}_{10} \ \overline{}_{19} \ \overline{}_{14}$

65

Hatching Chicks

How many *C*'s do you see?

67

Golden Egg Hunt

Can you help Morgan and Max find their way to the golden egg? Collect the letters along the correct path to find out the answer to the riddle.

Why shouldn't you tell an Easter egg a joke?
Because it might
⬜⬜⬜⬜⬜
⬜⬜!

Check...and Double Check

How many differences do you see between these pictures?

EGG-cellent

Each answer word contains a double G, just like EGG. Read through the clues to see how many you can crack open.

1. Ten went to the market ____ ____ ____ ____

2. Shake and move ____ ____ ____ ____ ____ ____

3. Man's best friend ____ ____ ____ ____ ____

4. Low clouds ____ ____ ____ ____ ____

5. Soaking wet ____ ____ ____ ____ ____

6. Tossing three balls at the same time

   ____ ____ ____ ____ ____ ____

7. Laughter ____ ____ ____ ____ ____ ____

8. Someone who runs

   ____ ____ ____ ____ ____ ____

9. Healthy greens

   ____ ____ ____ ____ ____ ____

10. Chicken or gold

   ____ ____ ____ ____ ____ ____

Superchallenge!

There are 30 objects hidden in this auditorium. Without clues or knowing what to look for, try to find them all. Good luck!

Illustrated by Paula Becker

Hidden WORDS

There are six words (not pictures!) hidden in the scene below.
Can you find CLOUDS, DAMP, PUDDLE, SHOWERS, STORMY, and WET?

Word Ladders

It's breakfast time! Can you help the early bird get to the worm? Use the clues to fill in the blanks. Each word is only one letter different from the word above it.

B I R D

(B) (I) (N) (D)

1. To tie up

2. A musical group

3. A magician's stick

4. To wish for something

5. A toad's skin might have one

6. Not hot, but not cold

W O R M

Hidden Pieces

Can you find the seven jigsaw pieces in this photo of jelly beans?

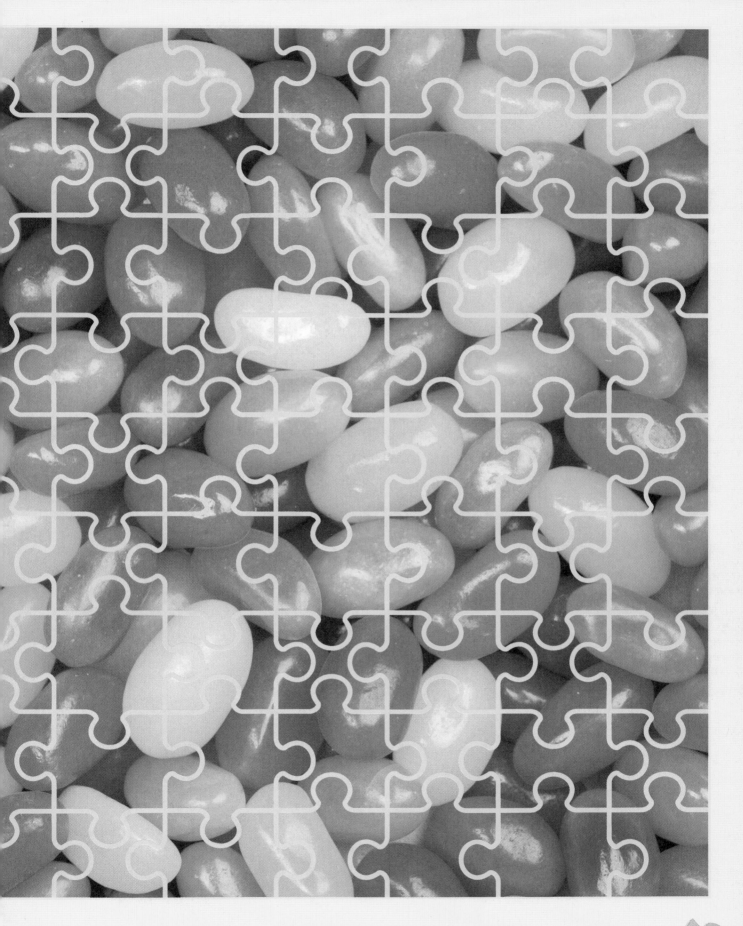

Easter Desserts

Carly and her brother, Eli, and her cousins Anthony and Kiera were excited about baking the desserts for their families' Easter celebration. Using the clues below, can you figure out which dessert each cousin baked and what flavor it was?

Use the chart to keep track of your answers. Put an **X** in each box that can't be true and an **O** in boxes that match.

	Pie	Muffins	Tart	Cake	Apple	Lemon	Coconut	Strawberry
Carly								
Anthony								
Kiera								
Eli								

1. Eli never bakes with coconut.
2. The girl who made muffins put strawberries in them.
3. Anthony made something with apples that was not a pie.
4. Kiera baked her favorite kind of cake.

Puzzle by Liza Keierleber

Test Your Memory

Quick! Study this picture for one minute. Then flip the page and see if you can answer the questions. No peeking!

Memory Test

Answer these questions about the picture on page 79. How well do you remember?

1. What color is the cat?
BLACK or GRAY

2. What is the weather like?
RAINY or SNOWY

3. How many tiers does the fountain have?
4 or 6

4. Which umbrella does NOT appear in the scene?

5. How many ducks are in the picture?
4 or 9

6. Besides the ducks, what else is swimming in the water?
TURTLES or FROGS

7. What color are the flowers?
PINK or WHITE

8. What was NOT shown in the picture?
A PATH or A CLOUD

80

Illustrated by Pat N. Lewis

Hello, Yellow!

Fourteen yellow items will fit into this grid. They can fit in just one way. Use the number of letters in each word as a clue to where it should go. Ready? Time to go for the gold— yellow gold, that is!

Word List

- ~~BEE~~
- SUN
- CORN
- TAXI
- CHICK
- LEMON
- BANANA
- BUTTER
- CANARY
- OMELET
- DAFFODIL
- GOLDFINCH
- SCHOOL BUS
- GRAPEFRUIT

B E E

There is more than meets the eye in this greenhouse. Can you find the hidden objects?

Illustrated by Jim Paillot

banana

scissors

dog bone

paintbrush

teacup

fork

light bulb

snail

doughnut

hammer

dragonfly

mouse

worm

seahorse

crayon

key

butterfly

frog

shoe

Word Ladders

It's dinner time! Can you help the bears catch some fish?
Use the clues to fill in the blanks. Each word is only one letter different from the word above it.

B E A R

1. What you do to a drum — B E A T

2. Good, better, _____

3. A girl's name, rhymes with Jess

4. An untidy area

5. To fail to hit the ball

6. Fog

7. Your hand can form this.

F I S H

Bunny Hop

Help the rabbit hop along the right path to reach his burrow. The symbols tell him which way to move.

move 1 space down

move 1 space up

move 1 space right

move 1 space left

Path 1 Path 2 Path 3 Path 4 Path 5 Path 6

Illustrated by Sherry Neidigh

Flower Flyby

Help the butterfly, bee, and hummingbird go from START to FINISH. Which one visits more flowers along the way?

FINISH

FINISH

FINISH

Illustrated by David Coulson

Every rabbit in the picture has one that looks just like it. Find all 10 matching pairs.

Illustrated by Dave Joly

Picture Puzzler

**Each bird on the top wire has a twin below with the same coloring.
Can you find each twin?**

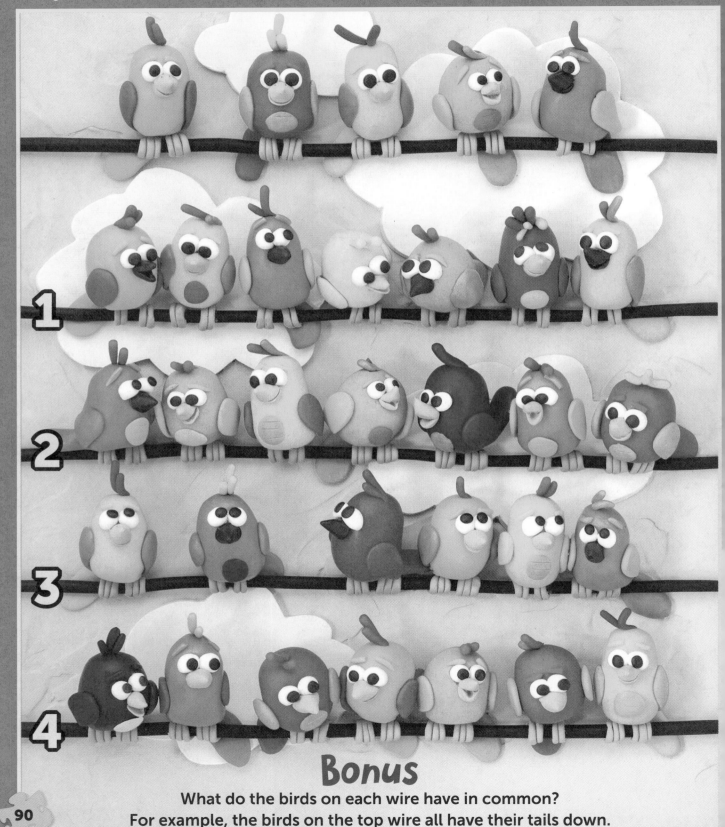

Bonus

What do the birds on each wire have in common?
For example, the birds on the top wire all have their tails down.

She Loves Me!

All the numbers on the daisy petals equal the sum in the center—all the numbers except one, that is. Can you pick off a single petal from each flower so that the sum of the remaining petals is correct?

Illustrated by Don Robison

These baby animals have been twisted and turned.
Can you figure out what each one is?

Tic Tac Row

Each of these kites has something in common with the other two kites in the same row. For example, in the first row across all three are box kites. Look at the other rows across, down, and diagonally. Can you tell what's alike in each row?

Planting Season

How many tomato plants can fit in a 9-foot-by-9-foot garden if the plants need to be 18 inches from one another, as well as 18 inches from the fence surrounding the plot?

Illustrated by Bill Colrus

9'

9'

18"

18"

18"

18"

Bird Is the Word

There are 20 HIDDEN BIRDS in this scene. Can you find them all?

Fowl Play

**What do you call
a very funny chicken?**
A comedi-hen

**What do you call a
very skinny bird?**
A narrow sparrow

**Why did the duck
become a spy?**
He was good at
quacking codes.

**What do you call a
seagull that flies over
a bay?**
A bagel

**What did the rooster
say to the cow?**
Cock-a-doodle-moo!

**Why did the ostrich
cross the road?**
To show he wasn't
chicken

**How did the chickens
leave the highway?**
They went through
the eggs-it.

Illustrated by Dave Klug

Carrot Maze

Skipper, Scoot, and Skitter are meeting in the park today. Find the path that each will take. Who will pick up the most carrots?

Hidden * Pieces

Can you find the seven jigsaw pieces in this photo of tulips?

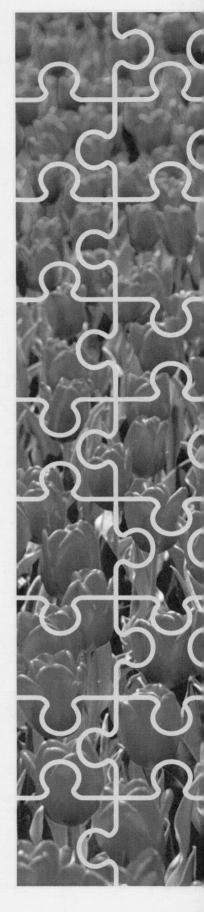

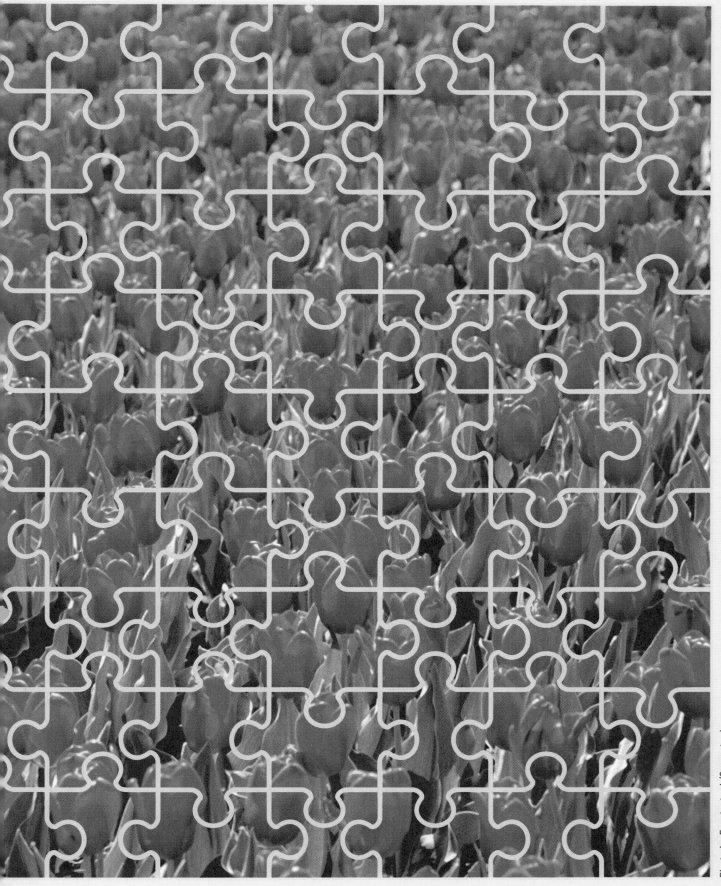

101

Letter Drop

Only six of the letters in the top line will work their way through this maze to land in the numbered squares at the bottom. When they get there, they will spell out the answer to the riddle.

R H A I P R O H C O K O P

1 2 3 4 5 6

What is a rabbit's favorite kind of music?

○ ○ ○
○ ○
○

Hidden Pictures
Spring Chickens

ladle

ice-cream bar

rocket ship

ruler

carrot

ice-cream cone

trowel

canoe

lemon

pennant

envelope

saltshaker

crescent moon

banana

slipper

Chick and Eggs
Nesting Chick

YOU WILL NEED: yarn, cardboard egg carton, scissors, white glue, half of an eggshell, paint or egg dye, paintbrush, hole punch, construction paper

Directions

1. Cut yarn into small sections. Then cut one cup from a cardboard egg carton. You can paint it or leave it plain.

2. Spread glue around inside of cup and attach yarn to look like straw.

3. Use paint or egg dye to color half an eggshell. Let dry.

4. Use a hole punch to make two paper circles for eyes. Cut out two triangles and fold each in half to make a beak.

5. Glue features in place. Then tuck the chick into its nest.

104

Decoupage Eggs

YOU WILL NEED: white glue, printed paper napkins, colored tissue paper, small paintbrush, plastic eggs, soda bottle caps

Directions

1. Tear a paper napkin or tissue paper into small pieces.

2. In a cup, mix two parts water to one part glue. Hold a piece of napkin or tissue paper over egg. Dip paintbrush into glue-and-water mix and paint over paper.

3. Cover half the egg this way, overlapping the edges of the paper. Place on a plastic bottle cap and let dry. Then cover the other half of the egg and let dry again.

Display each egg on a soda bottle cap or place them all in a basket.

Illustrated by Constanza Basaluzzo

Check . . . and Double Check

How many differences do you see between these pictures?

BLOOMING HUMOR

Flowers in the Puzzlemania garden do more than look pretty—they also crack codes! Count the number of petals on a flower. Then write the matching code letter in the center of the flower. Continue to fill in the flowers to find the answer to the riddle.

KEY

3 - E	9 - K
4 - D	10 - A
5 - I	11 - T
6 - R	12 - B
7 - H	13 - W
8 - G	14 - L

What did the dog do after he swallowed a firefly?

Illustrated by Jim Steck

Bird Bonanza

This puzzle's for the birds! Thirty-five birds to be exact. Look for them up, down, across, backwards, and diagonally. How many can you find?

Word List

~~ALBATROSS~~	KIWI
BLUEBIRD	LARK
CARDINAL	MAGPIE
CHICKADEE	NUTHATCH
CROW	ORIOLE
DUCK	OWL
EAGLE	PARAKEET
EGRET	PARROT
FLAMINGO	PELICAN
FLICKER	PIGEON
GNATCATCHER	QUAIL
GOLDFINCH	ROBIN
GROSBEAK	SPARROW
HAWK	TOUCAN
HERON	VIREO
IBIS	WARBLER
JUNCO	WOODPECKER
KINGFISHER	

R H G O L D F I N C H M O I B Y
E A W A G K J U N C O C Y I L Q
H W M L M W C T O R R A P Y U V
C K I B I S W O O D P E C K E R B
T L E A C H I C K A D E E B I R K
A C W T D R E H S I F G H I N R R
C F R R W E V N T N E G H F R A L
T L W O I Y O O E R I V Y N C A L
A I C S W E U L A N I D R A H L A
N C C S G C Y A G C A G R H O L Q
G K I I A S F F L A M I N G O A L
M E P N V I P Y E V G F R O V R Q
A R U U C W A R B L E R G R U R Q
G R O S B E A K R H T I D O C U A
P E L I C A N H E R O N B U L I L
I H C T A H T U N L O I V C C I L
E M P A R A K E E T N W E H V K

Illustrated by Wendy Wax

Hidden Pictures
Egg-cellent Discovery

kite

mitten

tennis racket

ring

heart

crown

needle

drinking straw

slice of pie

purse

scissors

button

teacup

sock

Tic Tac Row

Each of these birds has something in common with the other two birds in the same row. For example, in the top row across each bird is blue. Look at the other rows across, down, and diagonally. Can you tell what's alike in each row?

Illustrated by Carolina Farias

Bunnies

car

pear

bed

key

egg

mug

comb

pen

crayon

ice-cream bar

What is a bunny's favorite dance?

Cross out all the boxes in which the number cannot be evenly divided by three. Then write the leftover letters in the spaces to spell the answer.

31	33	17	7
T	H	K	L
49	**12**	**28**	**5**
E	I	R	J
90	**37**	**61**	**55**
P	W	O	O
13	**42**	**19**	**26**
K	H	A	B
23	**46**	**82**	**43**
S	P	R	G
3	**20**	**14**	**99**
O	B	L	P

_ _ _ _ _ _ _ _

Hidden Pictures
Butterfly Garden

Can you find these 12 items hidden with the butterflies?

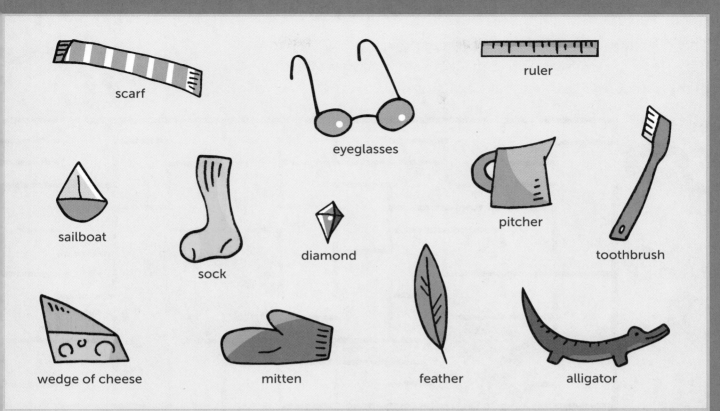

scarf

eyeglasses

ruler

sailboat

sock

diamond

pitcher

toothbrush

wedge of cheese

mitten

feather

alligator

Dot to Dot

Connect the dots from 1 to 21
to see a hungry crawler.

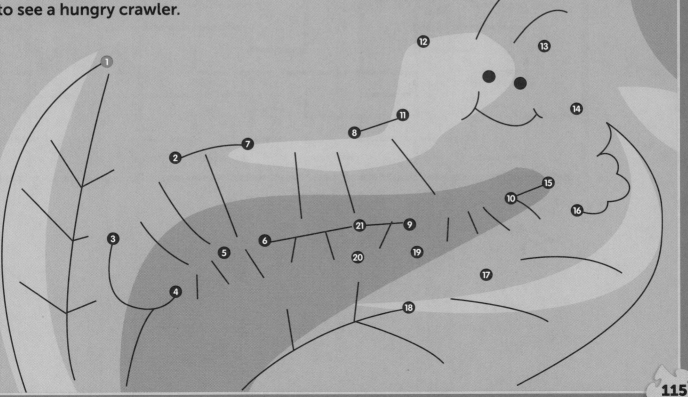

Ready, Set, Grow!

This community garden is growing in popularity. Can you help Rosemary meet her friend Tom so they can water their plants? Just one path will take her there.

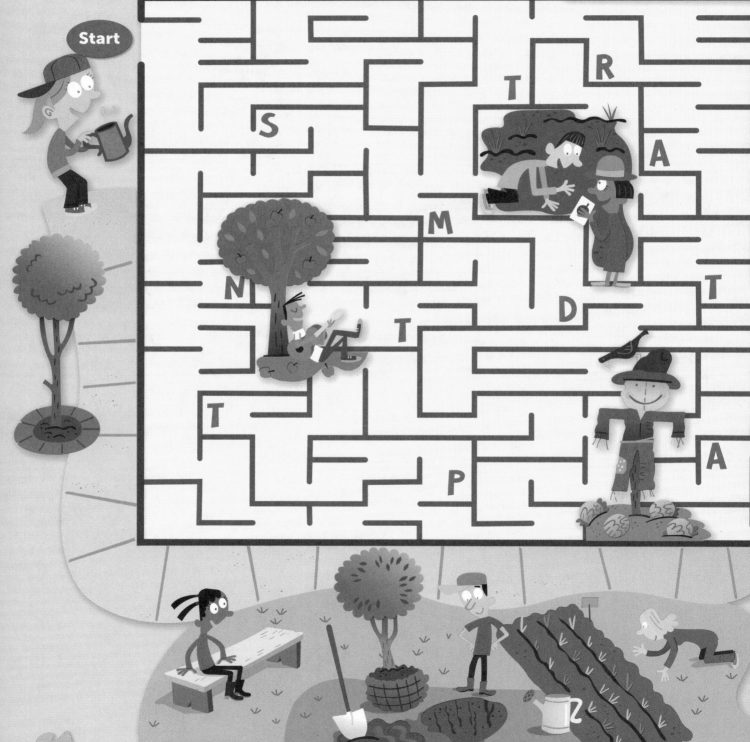

Start

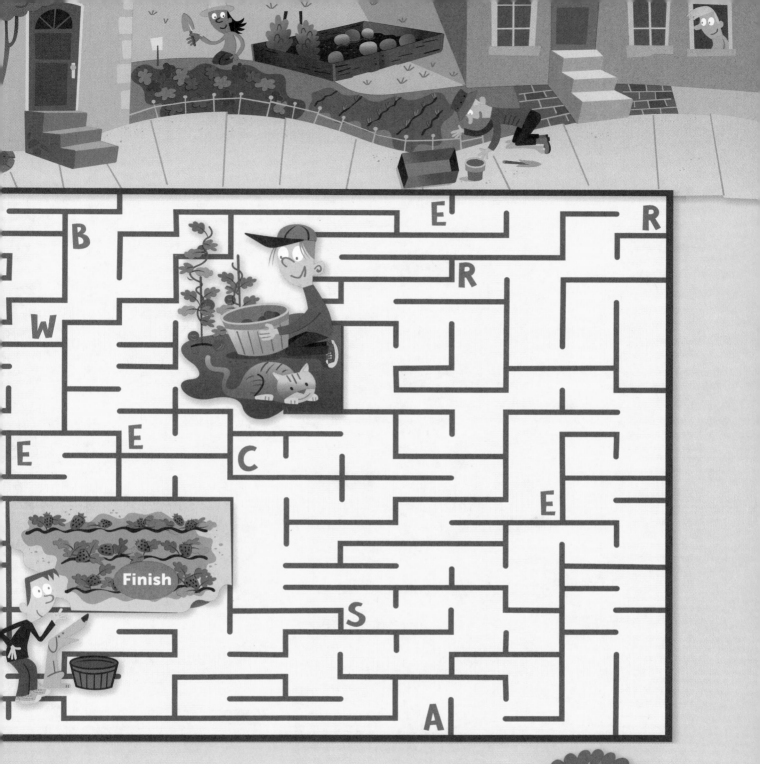

Bonus Puzzle

Once you've found the correct path, write the letters along it in order in the spaces below. They'll answer this riddle:

What is a scarecrow's favorite fruit?

_ _ _ _ _ _ _ _ _ _ _ _ _ _

Hidden Pictures
Pogo Rally

artist's brush

belt

harmonica

crescent moon

tube of toothpaste

light bulb

hat

doughnut

broccoli

118

needle

open book

bean

candle

toothbrush

banana

bow

purse

ruler

drinking straw

pencil

mug

domino

mitten

sandwich

fishhook

canoe

iron

clover

Illustrated by Susan Dahlman

119

Tree Trek

Start

Willow's friends built a brand-new tree house. She can't wait to climb aboard! Can you help Willow find the one path across her neighborhood that will take her there?

Finish

Button Blossoms

YOU WILL NEED: lightweight fabric, glue, poster board, scissors, chenille sticks, large, flat two-hole buttons

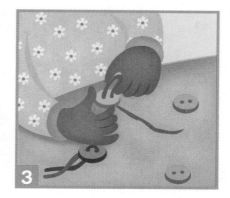

Directions

1. Spread glue on a piece of poster board and place fabric on top. Smooth out any wrinkles and let dry.

2. Cut out petal shapes from the fabric-covered board.

3. Insert a chenille stick up through one hole in a button and back down through the other hole. Twist ends together to make a stem.

4. Glue petals around underside edge of button. Let dry.

To welcome the holiday, make more flowers in a variety of colors and sizes.

Illustrated by Constanza Basaluzzo

Check...and Double Check

How many differences do you see between these pictures?

Illustrated by Anja Boretzki

Everyone is pitching in to turn this vacant lot into a park. But there is more than meets the eye here. Can you find the hidden objects?

Illustrated by Dave Klug

kite

toothbrush

canoe

magnifying glass

mitten

light bulb

ring

ladle

flashlight

seashell

shoe

hanger

paper clip

baseball bat

bow tie

banana

horseshoe

needle

slice of pie

envelope

sailboat

golf club

arrowhead

scarf

Match Maker

Illustrated by Dave Joly

Rabbit Maze

Start

Can you help this rabbit reach its room in the warren?
Find a clear path from START to FINISH. Better hop to it!

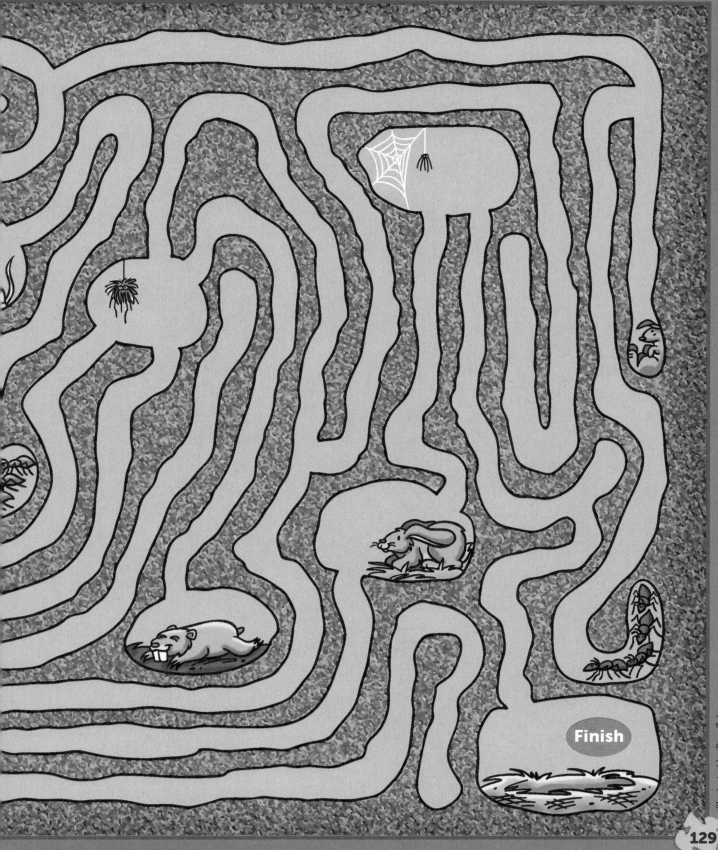

Finish

Illustrated by Ron Zalme

Digit Does It

The buzz in Inspector Digit's neighborhood is not good. Something has upset the delicate balance of the quiet suburban life. A neighbor's note should provide a clue about what's

Illustrated by John Nez

going on. Can you help the inspector decipher the cryptic clue so he can get in on a real "sting" operation? The first line reads, **"Dear Inspector Digit."**

__ __ __ __   __ __ __ __ __ __ __ __ __   __ __ __ __ __ ,
5 6 2 17   10 14 18 16 6 4 19 15 17   5 10 8 10 19

__ __ __ __   __ __ __   __ __ __ __ __ __ __
22 15 20 17   5 15 8   11 14 15 4 11 6 5

__ __ __ __   __ __   __ __ __ __ __ __ __ __ !
15 21 6 17   13 22   2 16 10 2 17 10 6 18

__ __   __ __ __ __   __ __ __ __   __ __ __ __ __ __ __ __ .
13 22   3 6 6 18   1 6 17 6   9 10 21 6 12 6 18 18

__   __ __ __   __ __ __ __ __ __   __ __ __
2   7 6 1   1 15 17 11 6 17 18   2 17 6

__ __ __ __ __   __ __ __ __ __ __ __ .   __ __   __ __ __ __ ,
18 19 10 12 12   13 10 18 18 10 14 8   10   1 15 14 19

__ __ __ __ __   __ __   __ __ __   __ __ __ __ __
5 17 15 14 6   15 14   3 20 19   1 15 20 12 5

__ __ __ __   __ __ __ __   __ __ __ __   __ __
12 10 11 6   22 15 20 17   9 6 12 16   19 15

__ __ __ __   __ __   __ __ __ __   __ __   __ __ __ __ .
7 10 14 5   13 22   12 2 18 19   A B   3 6 6 18

__ __ __ __ __   __ .   __ __ __ __ __ __
9 15 14 6 22   3   3 20 13 3 12 6

131

What's Wrong?

How many silly things can you find in this picture?

5 Candy Counter

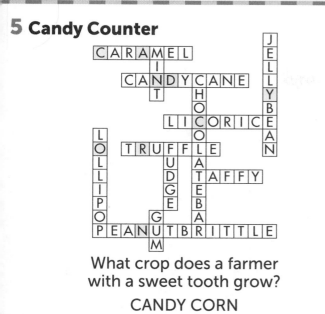

What crop does a farmer with a sweet tooth grow?

CANDY CORN

6 Hopping Egg Hunt

7 Meet the Beetles

8—9 Easter Basket Hunt

10—11 Check ... and Double Check

12—13 What's the Buzz?

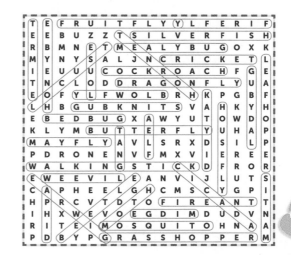

Answers

14–15 Spring Cleaning

PISTACHIOS   PECANS   CASHEWS
PEANUTS   BRAZIL NUTS   MACADAMIA
WALNUTS   CHESTNUTS   NUTS

16–17 Hidden Pieces

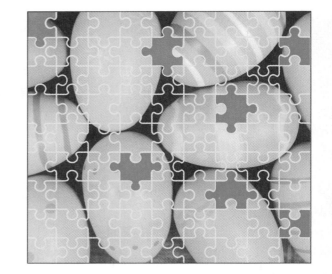

20–21 Splish Splash

22–23 Flower Q's

Flower Girl Power

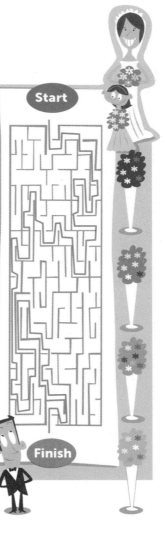

Start

Finish

Jumbled Flowers

LILY
TULIP
LILAC
VIOLET
DAFFODIL

Guess What?

ROSE   SUNFLOWER

Hidden Flowers

As Ter**r**y says, vanilla is better than chocolate.

A superhero **seldom** fails.

Ms. Go**rda** is your new teacher.

This **fir** is taller than it was last year.

On the **porch**, I don't get sunburned.

Flower or Not?

BLUEBELL
SNAPDRAGON
CHRYSANTHEMUM
RHODODENDRON
GLADIOLUS
CLEMATIS
HYDRANGEA
FOXGLOVE

Answers

26–27 Eggs for Breakfast

28–29 Wiggle Pictures

30 Hundred Hop

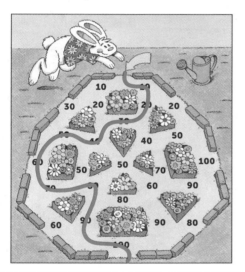

32–33 Shelled Out

34 Hippity-Zippity

What do you call a happy bunny?
A HOPTIMIST

35 Bunny Delivery

36–37 Matching Eggs

Answers

38–39 Win by a Hare

BEETS   TURNIP   ASPARAGUS

CELERY   ONION   BOK CHOY

CAULIFLOWER   RUTABAGA

40–41 Bloomin' Eggs

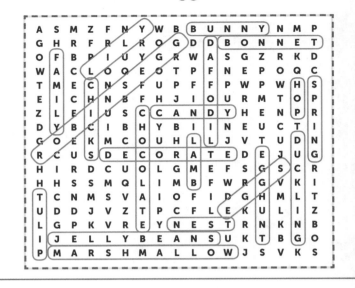

42–43 Eggscruciating

1. Why was the rooster so shy?
   HE LED A SHELL-TERED LIFE.

2. Why did Humpty Dumpty have a great fall?
   TO MAKE UP FOR A BAD SUMMER

3. What bird should you think of when an egg is thrown at you?
   DUCK!

44 Get on Board

46–47 Make a Rain Stick

48–49 Check . . . and Double Check

50 Double Cross

Why don't rabbits get hot in the summertime?
THEY HAVE HARE-CONDITIONING.

52–53 Rabbit Search

54–55 Kite Plight

51 Tic Tac Row

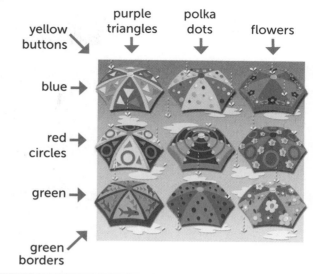

56 Puddle Play

57 Egg Factory

60–61 Bountiful Bouquets

Here is one solution.

4	9	8
11	7	3
6	5	10

Answers

64 Hop to the Finish Line

65 Bird Words

ROBIN
BLUE JAY
PARROT
SPARROW
HUMMINGBIRD

Why is the sky so high?
SO BIRDS WON'T BUMP THEIR HEADS

66–67 Hatching Chicks

The answer is 13.

68–69 Golden Egg Hunt

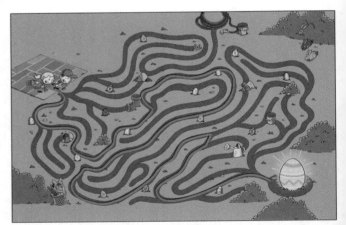

Why shouldn't you tell an Easter egg a joke?
Because it might CRACK UP!

70 Check . . . and Double Check

71 EGG-cellent

1. Ten went to the market   PIGGY
2. Shake and move   WIGGLE
3. Man's best friend   DOGGY
4. Low clouds   FOGGY
5. Soaking wet   SOGGY
6. Tossing three balls at the same time   JUGGL
7. Laughter   GIGGLE
8. Someone who runs   JOGGER
9. Healthy greens   VEGGIE
10. Chicken or gold   NUGGET

72–73 Superchallenge!

1. cane
2. seashell
3. pencil
4. ruler
5. ladle
6. feather
7. sock
8. ice-cream cone
9. snowman
10. magnifying glass
11. spool of thread
12. banana
13. glove
14. fork
15. bell
16. lock
17. carrot
18. pizza
19. boot
20. paper clip
21. snail
22. belt
23. funnel
24. celery
25. kite
26. tennis racket
27. nail
28. button
29. spoon
30. saltshaker

74 Hidden Words

75 Word Ladders

BIRD	BAND	WANT	WARM
BIND	WAND	WART	WORM

76–77 Hidden Pieces

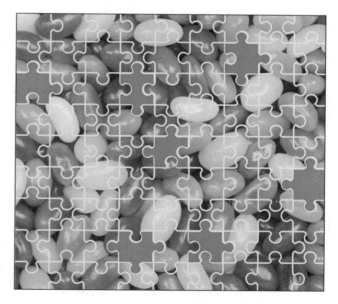

78 Easter Desserts

Carly: strawberry muffins

Anthony: apple tart

Kiera: coconut cake

Eli: lemon pie

80 Memory Test

1. GRAY
2. RAINY
3. 4
4. (bat image)
5. 9
6. FROGS
7. WHITE
8. A CLOUD

The Comedy Coop

1. BLUE JAYS
2. DRUMSTICKS
3. TWEETMENT
4. SPELLING BEES
5. WALKIE-TALKIES

Answers

81 Hello, Yellow!

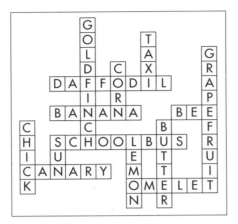

82—83 Seeing Green

84 Word Ladders

BEAR	BESS	MIST
BEAT	MESS	FIST
BEST	MISS	FISH

85 Bunny Hop

86—87 Flower Flyby

The BEE visits the most flowers along the way.

88—89 Match Maker

90 Picture Puzzler

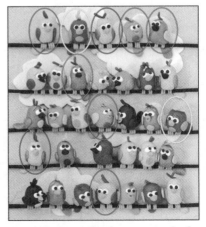

1. Two toes showing on each foot.
2. Spot on belly.
3. Looking up (and have closed beaks).
4. Have tan beaks.

91 She Loves Me!

17 flower: remove a 3 petal

22 flower: remove a 2 petal

31 flower: remove the 5 petal

25 flower: remove a 5 petal

34 flower: remove the 2 petal

18 flower: remove the 6 petal

92–93 Wiggle Pictures

polar bear cubs · lamb · puppy · calf · puma cubs · fawn

94 Tic Tac Row

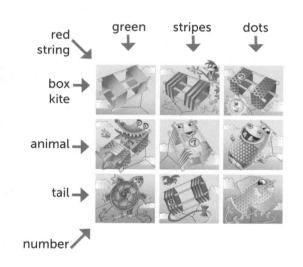

95 Planting Season

Go down any one side and continue making circles at 18-inch intervals as shown on the page. When you're done with the first row, continue measuring more rows in the same way. There will be room for 25 plants.

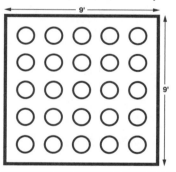

96–97 Bird Is the Word

98–99 Carrot Maze

SKIPPER picked up the most carrots.

Answers

100–101 Hidden Pieces

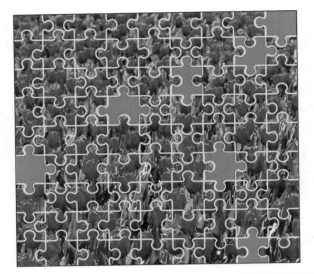

102 Letter Drop

What is a rabbit's favorite kind of music?
HIP HOP

103 Spring Chickens

106 Check . . . and Double Check

107 Blooming Humor

What did the dog do after he swallowed a firefly?

HE BARKED WITH DE-LIGHT!

108–109 Bird Bonanza

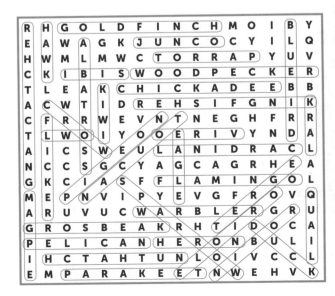

142

110 Egg-cellent Discovery

111 Tic Tac Row

112–113 Break-Dancing Bunnies

What is a Bunny's favorite dance?
HIP HOP

114–115 Butterfly Garden

116–117 Ready, Set, Grow!

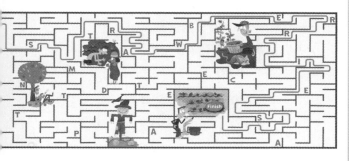

What is a scarecrow's
favorite fruit?
STRAWBERRIES

118–119 Pogo Rally

Answers

120 Tree Trek

122–123 Check . . . and Double Check

124–125 Park Project

126–127 Match Maker

128–129 Rabbit Maze

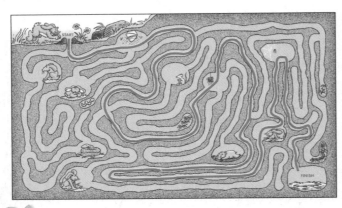

130–131 Digit Does It

Dear Inspector Digit,

Your dog knocked over my apiaries! My bees were hiveless. A few workers are still missing. I won't drone on but would like your help to find my last 23 bees.

Honey B. Bumble

a—2	g—8	n—14	u—20
b—3	h—9	o—15	v—21
c—4	i—10	p—16	w—1
d—5	k—11	r—17	y—22
e—6	l—12	s—18	
f—7	m—13	t—19	